Psittacosaurus

Written by Frances Swann
Illustrated by Pam Mara

Library of Congress Cataloging-in-Publication Data

Swann, Frances 1955–
  Psittacosaurus.

  Summary: Describes the physical characteristics and behavior of this horned-faced dinosaur that lived during the Cretaceous era.
  1. Psittacosaurus—Juvenile literature.
[1. Psittacosaurus 2. Dinosaurs] I. Mara, Pamela, ill. II. Title.
QE862.065S933 1988   567.9'7   87-37626
ISBN 0-86592-518-6

Rourke Enterprises, Inc.
Vero Beach, FL 32964

Quetzalcoatlus

Parasaurolphus

Deinosuchus

Corythasaurus

Spinosaurus

Oviraptor

Psittacosaurus

Pachycephalosaurus

Anatosaurus

Struthiomimus

Scolosaurus

Rutiodon

Psittacosaurus

The sun was already climbing in the sky over the distant purple hills as Psittacosaurus slowly awoke. He was hungry and not well rested, because it had been a strangely disturbing night. Thunder had rolled back and forth across the plain. Disturbed by it, the herd had sought out a higher shelter than usual.

The herd gradually assembled behind the older males. They protected the females and their young by keeping them in the middle. Then they moved off, walking quietly over the forest floor. Above them the yellow katsura and ginko leaves shaded them from the rising sun. The sharp smell of fallen ginko fruit filled Psittacosaurus's nostrils as he tested the air.

In a short time the herd reached a steep bank.
Here they slowed to let the youngsters cross it.
Psittacosaurus looked out over the hardwood forest
and across the plain. Below him he could see the great
delta that fanned out toward the sea. Several birds
soared on thermals above him. On the far side of the
plain he watched a huge herd of dinosaurs obscured by
a dust cloud moving slowly toward the forest edge.

Hungry now, the herd moved quickly toward their favorite feeding grounds. Every so often Psittacosaurus would grasp a passing cycad leaf, crop it with his powerful beak, and chew it as he walked.

Abruptly the herd stopped. Over the heads of the animals in front of him Psittacosaurus could see a small group of large Probactrosaurus. They turned to stare at the herd and then lumbered off a few feet to resume feeding. Noisily they raked down branches with their great thumb spikes. Then they settled again onto all fours to chew enormous amounts of foliage.

The herd moved on past them. They knew that despite their size the Probactrosaurus posed no danger.

At last the herd settled at a quiet feeding ground. Here they could eat in peace. Moving lightly from plant to plant, the herd grasped, chopped, and chewed the luscious green foliage. Palm-like cycads and big bennettitales leaves disappeared as they browsed. Psittacosaurus chewed idly as he watched the youngsters tackling the ferns of the undergrowth.

The heat of the sun was now beginning to penetrate the forest, and every so often, small lizards would dart in and out of view. A slight movement caught Psittacosaurus's eye. Coiled around a branch was a small snake watching him with unblinking eyes. Psittacosaurus moved past it on all fours, heading for some tasty flowering plants he had noticed.

The herd was now well satisified. With the warm sun on his back, Psittacosaurus rested.

Psittacosaurus felt wakeful and unsettled. Still chewing, he moved a little away from his herd. Suddenly, the peace of the forest was shattered by a commotion just yards away from Psittacosaurus. Frozen with fear, he dropped onto all fours among the tall ferns.

In front of him through the leaves, he could see a lone Deinonychus. The great creature was on its hind legs, its huge body towering over a Shamosaurus. The Deinonychus bellowed as the Shamosaurus swung its heavy tail club at the predator's ankles.

Deinonychus lunged repeatedly at the Shamosaurus, but the Shamosaurus was too agile for it. The Shamosaurus swung its tail club again. This time it drew blood, and the Deinonychus turned to escape. Psittacosaurus heard it crashing through the undergrowth as it fled.

When Psittacosaurus finally stood up again, the Shamosaurus had gone and the forest was calm.

Psittacosaurus rejoined his herd when they started to move. The forest seemed secure and safe again as they ambled on, travelling more slowly now in the sultry heat.

All of a sudden, little mammals startled from the undergrowth ran toward them. The herd, instantly sensing great danger, rose on their hind legs and ran panic-stricken, pursued by a large group of Deinonychus. Headlong they ran, terror driving them onward, gaining with every yard over their hunters.

Underfoot, decaying branches littered the, moss-covered ground, and young trees slowed their progress. Slowly the sounds of pursuit faded behind them.

Abruptly, the dark shade of the redwood trees gave way to the glare of sun on sand. The herd stood, flanks heaving with exhaustion. On a soft sand bank by the river, Psittacosaurus blinked in the bright light. Shaken by their narrow escape, the herd rested for a while. Keeping close to the edge of the forest, they moved on following the course of the river. Every so often a heron would flap off in front of them or a crocodile would silently slip back into the water. Otherwise all seemed peaceful, and Psittacosaurus began to relax.

Around a bend in the river, the herd came upon three female Bactrosaurus at a nest site. One female was covering her newly laid eggs with sand. The other two moved menacingly toward the herd. Quickly and warily, the herd skirted the nest site.

A sudden thrashing commotion at the river's edge caused the herd to stop and stare. In the churning water Psittacosaurus could see a pair of crocodiles twisting and turning as they tugged at a small dinosaur carcass. Not far from them was a flock of flamingos standing statue-like and unbothered.

The herd moved on, and the ground underfoot became wetter as they reached the edge of a shallow lake. Disturbed by their presence, a couple of basking turtles fell back into the water with a loud plop. In the shallow water Psittacosaurus could make out the darker shadows of darting fish.

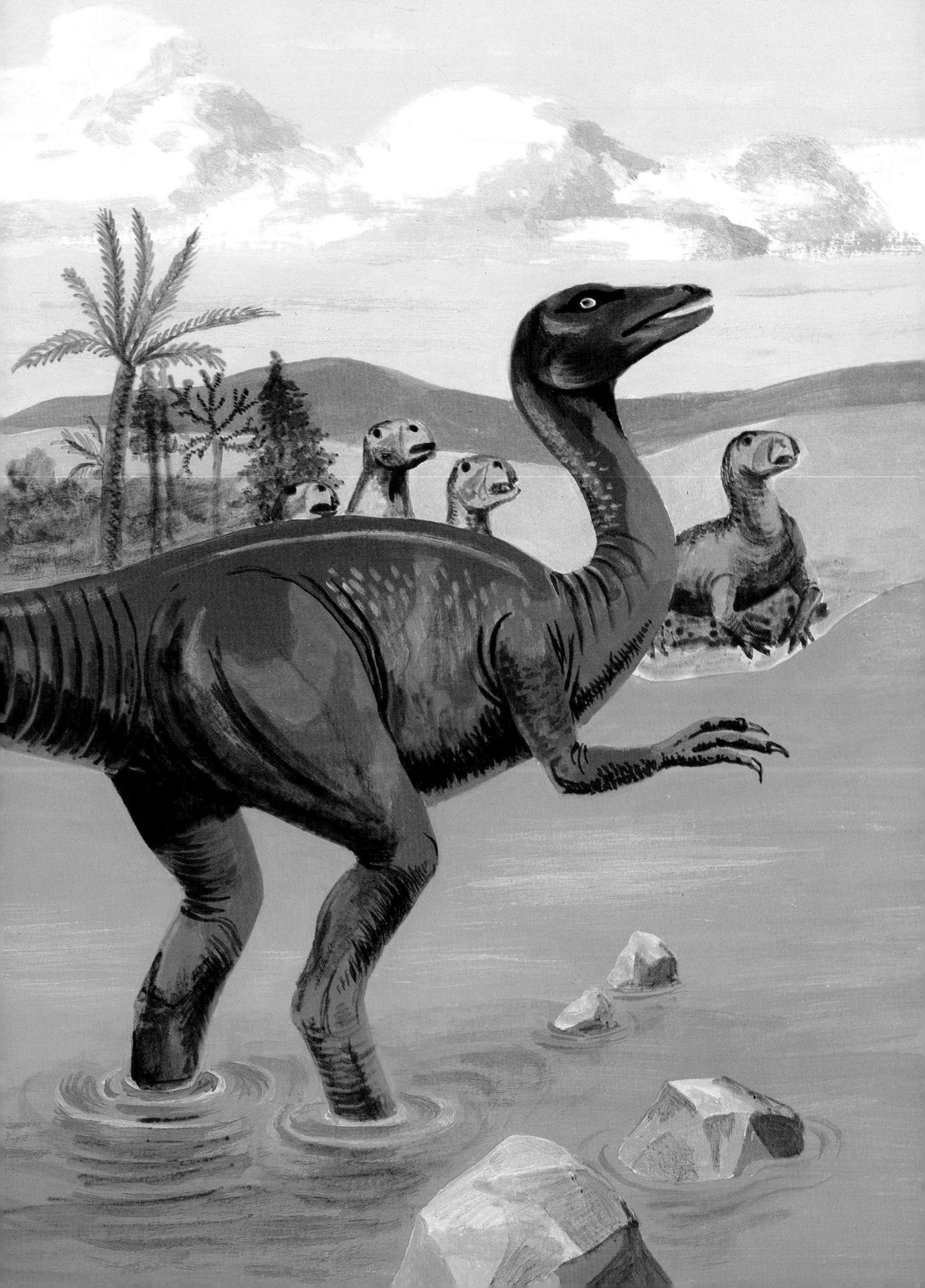

A slight sound made Psittacosaurus look up. Across the lake, a group of Segnosaurs splashed toward him through the shallows with their broad feet.

The Segnosaurs posed no threat, and the herd watched them curiously. In the distance Psittacosaurus noticed the vast dark shape of a Pterosaur soaring high above the water.

Slowly the herd turned away from the lake. The air was cooler now. Soon the light would begin to fade. The herd must feed again and find a safe resting place for the night. With a last glance at the lake, Psittacosaurus followed the others back into the shade of the forest. Pleasantly tired, he felt he would sleep well that night.

Psittacosaurus and the Cretaceous World

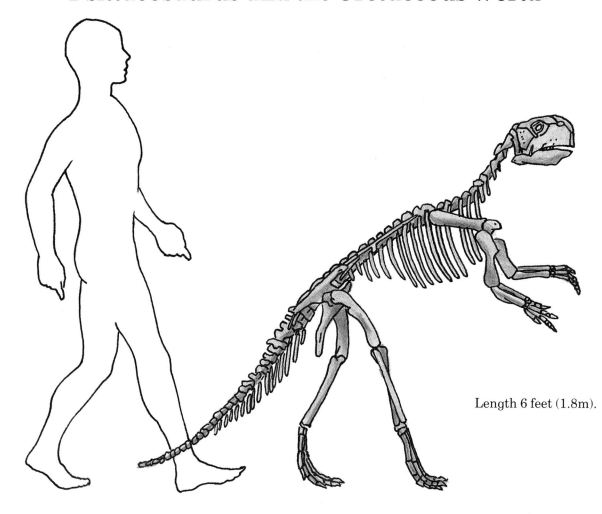

Length 6 feet (1.8m).

The skeleton of Psittacosaurus compared in size with a man

The Age of the Dinosaurs

The word *dinosaur* is derived from two Greek words meaning "terrible lizard." All the dinosaurs lived in the Mesozoic era, 225 to 64 million years ago, at a time when the continents were much closer to each other than today. At one time much of the land was one giant continent called Pangea. This great mass broke up over many millions of years — and segments drifted apart to become our present-day continents.

No human being has ever seen a dinosaur. Humans did not even appear on Earth until 2 to 3 million years ago. How then do we know so much about the dinosaurs?

Fossil Finds

Our knowledge has come from fossils that have been discovered all over the world. People have found fossil skeletons, eggs, nesting sites, tracks, dung, imprints of skin, and even mummified stomach contents. Every day new finds change our view of the dinosaurs and their world.

When Psittacosaurus Lived

The Mesozoic age is divided into three eras: Triassic, Jurassic, and Cretaceous. Psittacosaurus lived in the middle of the

Cretaceous era, which lasted from 135 to 64 million years ago. The word *Cretaceous* means "chalk". During this era great beds of chalk were laid down and the continents took on their present day shapes. At the start of the Cretaceous era the weather was mild, but by the end it was quite a lot colder.

The land was low-lying and it was a time of high sea levels with many deltas, rivers, lakes and swamps. Many new types of plants evolved during the Cretaceous era. Flowering plants appeared for the first time. By the end of the Cretaceous period existed many trees and plants that are familiar to us today.

All About Psittacosaurus

Psittacosaurus lived in Mongolia. He was a Ceratopian (horned face) dinosaur. It is probable he could use his hands both to grasp foliage and to walk. The long tail was used as a counterbalance when he ran; he would have relied on speed to escape predators.

The arrival of many new types of plants probably caused the evolution of Psittacosaurus's parrot-like beak, which enabled him to crop them.

Two of the tiniest dinosaur remains ever found were skulls of baby Psittacosaurus. The young would have been 16 inches (40cm) and 10 inches (25cm) long. They had large eyes, and their teeth were already worn from eating plant food.

Psittacosaurus probably laid eggs like Bractrosaurus, but no one knows how much parental care they gave their young.

Other Dinosaurs In This Book

Probactrosaurus
A 33 foot Mongolian dinosaur, very much like another dinosaur, Iguanadon. Probactrosaurus had large thumb spikes used for pulling down foliage to eat. These spikes may also have been used as a defensive weapon.

Deinonychus
A 10 foot dinosaur found in Montana. Although they lived at the same time, Psittacosaurus and Deinonychus would never actually have met. Fossils of Velociraptor, a dinosaur very similar to Deinonychus have been found in Mongolia. They show that Velociraptor lived only after Psittacosaurus had become extinct. They also show that similar predators hunted Psittacosaurus.

Shamosaurs
A Mongolian dinosaur so far only known from its skull. The skull shows clearly that Shamosaurus was an Ankylosaur of the type illustrated here. The tail club was an excellent weapon, heavy enough to disable a predator.

Bactrosaurus
A 20 foot Mongolian dinosaur with enormous sets of grinding teeth. So far, no remains of its forelimbs have been found, so we don't know how they looked. Fossilized nesting sites and baby dinosaurs of the same type have been found in North America.

Segnosaurus
A 20 foot Mongolian dinosaur with large broad-footed hind legs. Very possibly Segnosaurus was a fish-eating dinosaur with webbed feet.

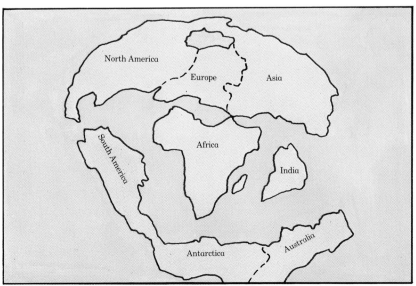

Map of the Cretaceous World